READING MADE EASY

BY: MICHELLE OWUSU-HEMENG

PRE-READING ACTIVITIES

SIGHT WORD HUNT

- BEFORE READING, HIGHLIGHT 5-10 SIGHT WORDS IN THE PASSAGE.
- HAVE STUDENTS PRACTICE READING THESE WORDS IN ISOLATION BEFORE THEY ENCOUNTER THEM IN THE PASSAGE.

PREVIEW AND PREDICT

- SHOW STUDENTS THE TITLE AND FIRST SENTENCE OF THE PASSAGE.
- ASK THEM TO PREDICT WHAT THE PASSAGE IS ABOUT.

ECHO READING

- READ THE PASSAGE ALOUD, EMPHASIZING FLUENCY AND EXPRESSION.
- HAVE STUDENTS REPEAT EACH SENTENCE AFTER YOU.

DURING-READING ACTIVITIES

CHORAL READING

- HAVE THE CLASS READ THE PASSAGE TOGETHER AS A GROUP.
- THIS HELPS STUDENTS PRACTICE PACING AND BUILDS CONFIDENCE.

PARTNER READING

- PAIR STUDENTS TO TAKE TURNS READING THE PASSAGE TO EACH OTHER.
- ENCOURAGE THEM TO PROVIDE POSITIVE FEEDBACK (E.G., "YOU READ THAT SMOOTHLY!" OR "GREAT EXPRESSION!").

Track with a Finger

- Encourage students to track each word with their finger as they read to build one-to-one correspondence.

Timed Reading

- Time students for one minute to see how many words they can read fluently.
- Repeat the activity over several days to track improvement.

Post-Reading Activities

Word Detective

- Have students go back through the passage and circle high-frequency words, rhyming words, or words with specific phonics patterns (e.g., "short a" or "blends").

RETELL THE STORY

- ASK STUDENTS TO RETELL THE PASSAGE IN THEIR OWN WORDS TO CHECK COMPREHENSION.
- USE DRAWINGS TO HELP VISUAL LEARNERS ILLUSTRATE KEY EVENTS.

ACT IT OUT

- TURN THE PASSAGE INTO A MINI PLAY! ASSIGN ROLES AND HAVE STUDENTS ACT OUT THE STORY USING THEIR VOICES TO EXPRESS DIFFERENT EMOTIONS OR ACTIONS.

FIND THE FLUENCY

- STUDENTS IDENTIFY PARTS OF THE PASSAGE THAT NEED EXPRESSION (E.G., EXCLAMATION POINTS OR DIALOGUE).

PRACTICE READING THESE SECTIONS WITH THE APPROPRIATE TONE AND EXPRESSION.

BUILD A SENTENCE

- WRITE SENTENCES FROM THE PASSAGE ON SENTENCE STRIPS, THEN CUT THEM INTO INDIVIDUAL WORDS.
- HAVE STUDENTS REARRANGE THE WORDS TO RECONSTRUCT THE SENTENCES.

EXTENSION ACTIVITIES

- CREATE A NEW ENDING
- ENCOURAGE STUDENTS TO COME UP WITH A NEW ENDING TO THE PASSAGE.
- THIS ACTIVITY PROMOTES CREATIVITY AND COMPREHENSION.

ILLUSTRATE THE PASSAGE

- HAVE STUDENTS DRAW A PICTURE THAT MATCHES THE PASSAGE.
- THEY CAN SHARE THEIR DRAWING AND EXPLAIN HOW IT RELATES TO WHAT THEY READ.

FLUENCY GRAPH

- CREATE A GRAPH TO TRACK WORDS PER MINUTE OVER TIME.
- CELEBRATE IMPROVEMENTS WITH STICKERS OR SMALL REWARDS TO MOTIVATE STUDENTS.

HOME CONNECTION

- SEND PASSAGES HOME FOR STUDENTS TO PRACTICE WITH FAMILY MEMBERS.

LEVEL 1 STORIES: TO DEVELOP THEIR READING FLUENCY. THESE PASSAGES FOCUS ON SIMPLE SENTENCES, REPETITION, AND HIGH-FREQUENCY SIGHT WORDS.

ANIMAL FRIENDS

"THE BIG DOG"

THE DOG IS BIG.

THE DOG RUNS FAST.

THE DOG LIKES TO PLAY.

I LIKE THE BIG DOG!

"FUNNY CAT"

THE CAT IS ON THE MAT.

THE CAT IS IN THE HAT.

THE CAT IS SO FUNNY!

I LIKE THE FUNNY CAT.

"LOOK AT THE BIRD"

LOOK AT THE BIRD.

THE BIRD IS RED.

THE BIRD CAN FLY.

I SEE THE BIRD IN THE TREE.

EVERYDAY LIFE

"MY TOY CAR"

I HAVE A TOY CAR.

IT IS RED AND BLUE.

MY CAR GOES FAST!

I LOVE MY TOY CAR.

"THE BIG BOX"

I SEE A BIG BOX.

WHAT IS IN THE BOX?

A BEAR IS IN THE BOX!

I PLAY WITH THE BIG BOX.

"TIME TO EAT"

I LIKE TO EAT.

I EAT AN APPLE.

I EAT A BANANA.

YUM! I LIKE TO EAT.

SEASONS AND NATURE

"THE SUNNY DAY"

THE SUN IS OUT.

I PLAY IN THE SUN.

THE SUN IS HOT.

I LIKE SUNNY DAYS.

"A RAINY DAY"

IT IS RAINY TODAY.

I SEE THE BIG RAIN.

I JUMP IN A PUDDLE.

I LIKE THE RAINY DAY!

"IN THE SNOW"

I SEE THE SNOW.

THE SNOW IS COLD.

I MAKE A SNOWMAN.

I LOVE THE SNOW!

IMAGINATIVE PLAY

"MY RED BALLOON"

HAVE A RED BALLOON.
IT GOES UP, UP, UP!
I HOLD THE STRING TIGHT.
I LOVE MY RED BALLOON.

"A ROCKET SHIP"

I SEE A ROCKET SHIP.

IT GOES ZOOM, ZOOM, ZOOM!

THE ROCKET IS SO FAST.

I WANT TO RIDE THE ROCKET.

"THE LITTLE TRAIN"

THE TRAIN IS ON THE TRACK.

CHOO, CHOO, GOES THE TRAIN!

THE TRAIN IS SO FUN.

I RIDE THE LITTLE TRAIN.

CELEBRATIONS

"HAPPY BIRTHDAY"

IT IS MY BIRTHDAY!

I HAVE A CAKE.

I BLOW OUT THE CANDLES.

I LIKE MY BIRTHDAY.

"THE BIG PARTY"

WE HAVE A BIG PARTY.

I SEE MY FRIENDS.

WE PLAY AND EAT CAKE.

I LOVE THE BIG PARTY!

"A FUN PICNIC"

WE GO TO THE PARK.

WE SIT ON A BIG MAT.

I EAT A SANDWICH.

I LIKE THE FUN PICNIC.

LEVEL 2: FEATURES OF THESE PASSAGES: IMPROVE THEIR READING FLUENCY. THESE PASSAGES FOCUS ON SIMPLE SENTENCE STRUCTURES, SIGHT WORDS, AND ENGAGING TOPICS

ANIMAL ADVENTURES

"SAM THE CAT"

Sam the cat sat on a mat.

He saw a rat and ran.

The rat hid in a hat.

Sam sat and waited.

"BENNY THE BUNNY"

Benny the Bunny hops all day. He jumps over logs and plays in hay. Benny loves to eat carrots, too. What else do bunnies like to do?

"THE BUSY BEE"

A BEE BUZZES BY THE TREE.
IT LANDS ON A BRIGHT RED ROSE.
THE BEE TAKES NECTAR AND FLIES AWAY.
WHAT A BUSY LITTLE BEE!

EVERYDAY FUN

"A DAY AT THE PARK"

I RUN TO THE SLIDE.

I CLIMB TO THE TOP.

DOWN I GO SO FAST! THE PARK IS SO MUCH FUN!

"THE BIG RED BALL"

I KICK THE BIG RED BALL.

IT ROLLS PAST THE WALL.

MY DOG RUNS AFTER IT.

WE LOVE TO PLAY WITH THE BALL!

"TOM'S NEW HAT"

TOM HAS A NEW HAT.

IT IS BLUE WITH A YELLOW STAR.

HE WEARS IT TO THE STORE.

"I LOVE MY NEW HAT!" SAYS TOM.

NATURE WONDERS

"A WALK IN THE WOODS"

I SEE A BIRD IN A TREE.

IT SINGS A SWEET SONG FOR ME.

I SEE A SQUIRREL WITH A NUT.

IT RUNS TO ITS LITTLE HUT.

"RAINY DAY FUN"

THE RAIN FALLS ON MY ROOF.

DRIP, DROP, DRIP, DROP.

PUT ON MY BOOTS AND COAT.

SPLASH! I JUMP IN A PUDDLE!

"STARS AT NIGHT"

AT NIGHT, I SEE THE STARS.

THEY TWINKLE IN THE DARK SKY.

THE MOON SHINES BIG AND BRIGHT.

I LOVE LOOKING AT THE NIGHT SKY.

IMAGINATIVE STORIES

"THE LOST SOCK"

I LOST MY SOCK UNDER THE BED.

I LOOK BEHIND THE DOOR INSTEAD.

I SEE IT BY THE CHAIR.

HOORAY! MY SOCK IS THERE!

"MAGIC KITE"

MY KITE FLIES HIGH IN THE SKY.

THE WIND TAKES IT UP, UP, UP.

IT LOOKS LIKE IT CAN TOUCH THE CLOUDS.

WHAT A MAGICAL KITE!

"THE LITTLE BOAT"

I HAVE A BOAT THAT SAILS THE SEA.

IT FLOATS SO FAST AND CARRIES ME.

WE GO PAST FISH, TURTLES, AND WHALES.

MY BOAT LOVES TO FOLLOW THE SAILS.

CELEBRATIONS AND SEASONS

"SPRING FLOWERS"

THE FLOWERS BLOOM IN SPRING.

RED, YELLOW, AND BLUE.

I PICK A FLOWER FOR MY MOM.

"THANK YOU!" SHE SAYS WITH A BIG SMILE

"A SNOWY DAY"

SNOW FALLS ON THE GROUND.

I MAKE A SNOWMAN BIG AND ROUND.

I GIVE HIM A SCARF AND HAT.

NOW HE LOOKS JUST LIKE THAT!

"THE BIG BIRTHDAY CAKE"

TODAY IS MY BIRTHDAY! I HAVE A BIG CAKE WITH CANDLES ON TOP. I BLOW OUT THE CANDLES AND MAKE A WISH. MY BIRTHDAY IS THE BEST DAY EVER!

LEVEL 3 – THESE PASSAGES ARE SLIGHTLY MORE ADVANCED, WITH LONGER SENTENCES, VARIED VOCABULARY, AND TOPICS THAT ENGAGE GROWING READERS

ANIMAL TALES

"THE CLEVER FOX"

THE FOX WAS HUNGRY. HE LOOKED FOR FOOD IN THE FOREST.

HE SAW A RABBIT AND TRIED TO CATCH IT.

BUT THE RABBIT WAS TOO FAST! THE FOX RAN AWAY.

"MAX AND THE DUCKS"

MAX WENT TO THE POND TO FEED THE DUCKS. HE THREW BREAD CRUMBS INTO THE WATER. THE DUCKS QUACKED AND FLAPPED THEIR WINGS. MAX LAUGHED AND FED THEM SOME MORE.

"BUSY ANTS"

ANTS WORK ALL DAY. THEY CARRY LEAVES AND TINY CRUMBS TO THEIR HILL. THE QUEEN ANT WATCHES OVER THE NEST. ANTS ARE SMALL BUT VERY STRONG!

OUTDOOR ADVENTURES

"THE BIG HILL"

JAKE AND ELLA CLIMBED A BIG HILL. IT WAS HARD WORK, BUT THEY DIDN'T STOP. AT THE TOP, THEY SAW A BLUE SKY AND GREEN TREES. "THIS VIEW IS AMAZING!" SAID JAKE.

"A DAY AT THE BEACH"

WE WENT TO THE BEACH. I PLAYED IN THE SAND AND BUILT A TALL CASTLE. MY SISTER FOUND SHINY SHELLS NEAR THE WATER. WE SWAM UNTIL THE SUN WENT DOWN.

"THE KITE"

MY KITE FLEW HIGH IN THE SKY. THE WIND CARRIED IT UP, UP, UP! SUDDENLY, THE STRING BROKE, AND THE KITE FLEW AWAY. "OH NO!" I SAID, BUT IT WAS FUN WHILE IT LASTED.

EVERYDAY LIFE

"THE LOST PENCIL"

MIA COULDN'T FIND HER PENCIL. SHE LOOKED UNDER THE TABLE AND BEHIND THE CHAIR. "HERE IT IS!" SAID HER BROTHER. IT WAS HIDING IN HER BACKPACK ALL ALONG.

"GRANDMA'S COOKIES"

GRANDMA MAKES THE BEST COOKIES.

SHE MIXES FLOUR, SUGAR, AND CHOCOLATE CHIPS IN A BIG BOWL.

WHEN THE COOKIES ARE DONE, THE HOUSE SMELLS SO GOOD.

I CAN'T WAIT TO EAT THEM!

"THE RAINY DAY"

IT RAINED ALL DAY, SO WE STAYED INSIDE. I PLAYED BOARD GAMES WITH MY BROTHER. WE READ BOOKS AND WATCHED A MOVIE. RAINY DAYS CAN BE FUN, TOO!

IMAGINATIVE STORIES

"THE MAGIC SHOES"

SARAH FOUND A PAIR OF SHINY RED SHOES. WHEN SHE PUT THEM ON, SHE COULD JUMP REALLY HIGH! SHE JUMPED OVER A FENCE AND INTO A FIELD OF FLOWERS. "THESE SHOES ARE AMAZING!" SHE SAID.

"TIM'S BIG IDEA"

TIM WANTED TO BUILD A ROBOT. HE USED BOXES, WIRES, AND BUTTONS. WHEN HE PRESSED A SWITCH, THE ROBOT MOVED! "IT WORKS!" TIM SHOUTED WITH JOY.

"THE TALKING DOG"

I MET A DOG WHO COULD TALK.

"WHAT'S YOUR NAME?" I ASKED.

"MY NAME IS BUDDY," SAID THE DOG.

"LET'S GO PLAY!"

SEASONAL FUN

"SPRING FLOWERS"

In spring, flowers bloom in bright colors. Bees buzz around the garden, collecting nectar. The air smells fresh, and the sun feels warm. Spring is my favorite season.

"THE SNOWY DAY"

SNOW FELL ALL NIGHT, COVERING THE GROUND IN WHITE.

I PUT ON MY COAT AND BOOTS AND RAN OUTSIDE.

I MADE A SNOWMAN WITH A HAT AND A SCARF.

SNOW DAYS ARE THE BEST!

"HALLOWEEN NIGHT"

ON HALLOWEEN, WE DRESSED UP AND WENT TRICK-OR-TREATING. I WAS A PIRATE, AND MY SISTER WAS A PRINCESS. WE KNOCKED ON DOORS AND SAID, "TRICK OR TREAT!" OUR BAGS WERE FULL OF CANDY BY THE END OF THE NIGHT.

Level 1 Sight Words

all
am
are
at
ate
be
black
brow
in
but
came
did
do
eat
four
get
good
have
he
into
like
must
new
no
now
on
our

out
please
pretty
ran
ride
saw
say
she so
soon
that
there
they
this
too
under
want
was
well
went
what
white
who
will
with
yes

Level 2 Sight Words

LIST #1

all
I
an
go
my
no
be
at
sat
yes

LIST #2

are
can
had
am
into
let
day
did
has
me

LIST #3

little
big
as
see
we
run
was
saw
two
too

LIST #4

will
ran
this
up
down
Mrs.
Mr.
Miss
on
ask

LIST #5

new
old
about
from
girl
have
came
come
get
off

LIST #6

he
away
boy
its
do
by
out
sun
they
she

YLevel 3 Sight Words

a	have	he
can	is	like
and	jump	little
come	my	no
are	one	of
for	put	saw
big	the	this
go	want	to
has	what	we
I	you	with

about	after	good
because	before	many
here	call	near
look	do	off
me	earth	people
play	father	right
said	give	that
see	her	two
she	know	under
try	large	very

Meet Michelle Hemeng
A Voice of Empowerment and Inspiration!

Hello, my name is Michelle Hemeng, and I am a passionate first-grade teacher committed to nurturing young minds and ensuring that no child is ever left behind. As an educator, I believe in the power of literacy to transform lives and open doors to endless possibilities. Through every lesson I teach, I aim to instill not only a love for reading and learning but also a sense of pride and confidence in every child, especially low income, Title 1 schools.

My mission extends far beyond the classroom walls. As an African-American woman in a leadership role, I am dedicated to being a living example of what is possible when determination, hard work, and perseverance intersect. I believe that every young girl—regardless of background or circumstance—has the potential to break through barriers and redefine the future. It is my hope that through the stories I share in my children's literacy books, young readers can see themselves reflected in powerful, positive narratives that challenge stereotypes and inspire greatness.

I am not just a teacher; I am a mentor, an advocate, and a role model for children who need to see that their dreams are achievable. Through my work, I strive to help young minds recognize that they too can rise above societal limitations, overcome obstacles, and chart their own paths to success. It is possible for them to dream big, work hard, and create a world where they are the leaders of tomorrow.

Let us journey together—empowering young readers to believe in themselves, embrace their unique identities, and chase their dreams with unwavering confidence

www.ingramcontent.com/pod-product-compliance
Lightning Source LLC
LaVergne TN
LVHW081317060526
838201LV00006B/183